This boo

Go See
≡THE≡
WORLD!

I ♥ travel

Location:

DATE:

WEATHER:

TODAYS ACTIVITY:

THE MOST INTERESTING I SAW:

TODAY I ATE:

TODAY I LEARNED:

Sketch what you saw:

RATE YOUR DAY:

TODAY'S FAVORITE MEMORY:

TODAY I AM GRATEFUL FOR:

Location: _____

_____

N
W E
S

DATE: _____

WEATHER:

☀ ⛅ ☁ 🌧

TODAYS ACTIVITY: _____

THE MOST INTERESTING I SAW: _____

TODAY I ATE: _____

TODAY I LEARNED: _____

Sketch what you saw:

RATE YOUR DAY:

TODAY'S FAVORITE MEMORY:

TODAY I AM GRATEFUL FOR:

Location: _____   DATE: _____

```
      N
 W  ✦  E                           WEATHER:
      S
```
_____

_____

_____

TODAYS ACTIVITY: _____

_____

_____

_____

_____

_____

- -

THE MOST INTERESTING I SAW: _____

_____

_____

- -

TODAY I ATE: _____

_____

_____

- -

TODAY I LEARNED: _____

_____

_____

_____

_____

_____

Sketch what you saw:

RATE YOUR DAY:

TODAY'S FAVORITE MEMORY:

TODAY I AM GRATEFUL FOR:

Location:

DATE:

N
W E
S

WEATHER:

TODAYS ACTIVITY:

THE MOST INTERESTING I SAW:

TODAY I ATE:

TODAY I LEARNED:

Sketch what you saw:

RATE YOUR DAY:

TODAY'S FAVORITE MEMORY:

TODAY I AM GRATEFUL FOR:

Location: _____   **DATE:** _____

N   _____

W ✦ E

S

WEATHER:

TODAYS ACTIVITY: _____

THE MOST INTERESTING I SAW: _____

TODAY I ATE: _____

TODAY I LEARNED: _____

Sketch what you saw:

RATE YOUR DAY:

TODAY'S FAVORITE MEMORY:

TODAY I AM GRATEFUL FOR:

Location: _____

DATE: _____

N
W — E
S

WEATHER:

TODAYS ACTIVITY: _____

- - - - - - - - - - - - - - - -

THE MOST INTERESTING I SAW: _____

- - - - - - - - - - - - - - - -

TODAY I ATE: _____

- - - - - - - - - - - - - - - -

TODAY I LEARNED: _____

Sketch what you saw:

RATE YOUR DAY:

TODAY'S FAVORITE MEMORY:

TODAY I AM GRATEFUL FOR:

Location:

N
W E
S

WEATHER:

TODAYS ACTIVITY:

THE MOST INTERESTING I SAW:

TODAY I ATE:

TODAY I LEARNED:

Sketch what you saw:

RATE YOUR DAY:

TODAY'S FAVORITE MEMORY:

TODAY I AM GRATEFUL FOR:

Location: _____

N
W ✦ E
S
_____
_____

WEATHER:

☀ ⛅ ☁ 🌧

●●

TODAYS ACTIVITY: _____

_____
_____
_____
_____
_____
_____

- -

THE MOST INTERESTING I SAW: _____

_____
_____
_____

- -

TODAY I ATE: _____

_____
_____
_____

- -

TODAY I LEARNED: _____

_____
_____
_____
_____
_____

Sketch what you saw:

RATE YOUR DAY:

TODAY'S FAVORITE MEMORY:

TODAY I AM GRATEFUL FOR:

Location: _____ DATE: _____

N
W — E   _____ WEATHER: ☀ ⛅ ☁ 🌧
S   _____

TODAYS ACTIVITY: _____
_____
_____
_____
_____
_____

THE MOST INTERESTING I SAW: _____
_____
_____
_____

TODAY I ATE: _____
_____
_____
_____

TODAY I LEARNED: _____
_____
_____
_____
_____

Sketch what you saw:

RATE YOUR DAY:

TODAY'S FAVORITE MEMORY:

TODAY I AM GRATEFUL FOR:

Location: _____

DATE: _____

N
W — E
S

WEATHER:

TODAYS ACTIVITY: _____
_____
_____
_____
_____
_____

THE MOST INTERESTING I SAW: _____
_____
_____
_____

TODAY I ATE: _____
_____
_____

TODAY I LEARNED: _____
_____
_____
_____
_____

Sketch what you saw:

RATE YOUR DAY:

TODAY'S FAVORITE MEMORY:

TODAY I AM GRATEFUL FOR:

Location: _____

DATE: _____

N
W E
S
_____
_____

WEATHER:

TODAYS ACTIVITY: _____
_____
_____
_____
_____
_____

- - - - - - - - - - - - - - - - - - - -

THE MOST INTERESTING I SAW: _____
_____
_____
_____

- - - - - - - - - - - - - - - - - - - -

TODAY I ATE: _____
_____
_____
_____

- - - - - - - - - - - - - - - - - - - -

TODAY I LEARNED: _____
_____
_____
_____
_____
_____

Sketch what you saw:

RATE YOUR DAY:

TODAY'S FAVORITE MEMORY:

TODAY I AM GRATEFUL FOR:

Location: _____

DATE: _____

WEATHER:

N
W E
S

TODAYS ACTIVITY: _____

THE MOST INTERESTING I SAW: _____

TODAY I ATE: _____

TODAY I LEARNED: _____

Sketch what you saw:

RATE YOUR DAY:

TODAY'S FAVORITE MEMORY:

TODAY I AM GRATEFUL FOR:

Location:

DATE:

N
W · E
S

WEATHER:

TODAYS ACTIVITY:

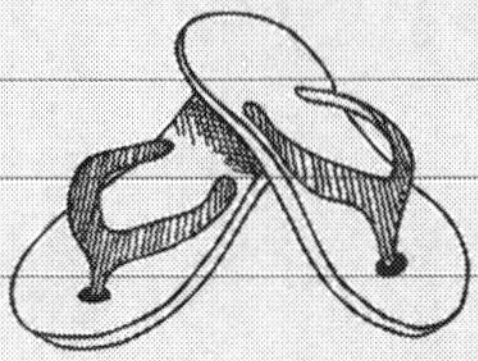

THE MOST INTERESTING I SAW:

TODAY I ATE:

TODAY I LEARNED:

Sketch what you saw:

RATE YOUR DAY:

TODAY'S FAVORITE MEMORY:

TODAY I AM GRATEFUL FOR:

Location:

DATE:

N
W E
S

WEATHER:

TODAYS ACTIVITY:

THE MOST INTERESTING I SAW:

TODAY I ATE:

TODAY I LEARNED:

Sketch what you saw:

RATE YOUR DAY:

TODAY'S FAVORITE MEMORY:

TODAY I AM GRATEFUL FOR:

Location: _____ **DATE:** _____

N
W — E
S
_____

_____

WEATHER:

TODAYS ACTIVITY: _____

THE MOST INTERESTING I SAW: _____

TODAY I ATE: _____

TODAY I LEARNED: _____

Sketch what you saw:

RATE YOUR DAY:

TODAY'S FAVORITE MEMORY:

TODAY I AM GRATEFUL FOR:

Location: _____

DATE: _____

N
W ✦ E
S

WEATHER: ☀ ⛅ ☁ 🌧

TODAYS ACTIVITY: _____
_____
_____
_____
_____
_____

THE MOST INTERESTING I SAW: _____
_____
_____

TODAY I ATE: _____
_____
_____

TODAY I LEARNED: _____
_____
_____
_____
_____
_____

Sketch what you saw:

RATE YOUR DAY:

TODAY'S FAVORITE MEMORY:

TODAY I AM GRATEFUL FOR:

Location: _____

DATE: _____

N
W E
S

WEATHER:

TODAYS ACTIVITY: _____

THE MOST INTERESTING I SAW: _____

TODAY I ATE: _____

TODAY I LEARNED: _____

Sketch what you saw:

RATE YOUR DAY:

TODAY'S FAVORITE MEMORY:

TODAY I AM GRATEFUL FOR:

Location: _____

DATE: _____

WEATHER:

```
N
W     E
S
```

TODAYS ACTIVITY: _____

THE MOST INTERESTING I SAW: _____

TODAY I ATE: _____

TODAY I LEARNED: _____

Sketch what you saw:

RATE YOUR DAY:

TODAY'S FAVORITE MEMORY:

TODAY I AM GRATEFUL FOR:

Location: _____

```
      N
  W --+-- E
      S
```
_____
_____

WEATHER:

TODAYS ACTIVITY: _____

THE MOST INTERESTING I SAW: _____

TODAY I ATE: _____

TODAY I LEARNED: _____

Sketch what you saw:

RATE YOUR DAY:

TODAY'S FAVORITE MEMORY:

TODAY I AM GRATEFUL FOR:

Location: _____

DATE: _____

WEATHER:

TODAYS ACTIVITY: _____

THE MOST INTERESTING I SAW: _____

TODAY I ATE: _____

TODAY I LEARNED: _____

Sketch what you saw:

RATE YOUR DAY:

TODAY'S FAVORITE MEMORY:

TODAY I AM GRATEFUL FOR:

Location:

DATE:

N
W E
S

WEATHER:

TODAYS ACTIVITY:

THE MOST INTERESTING I SAW:

TODAY I ATE:

TODAY I LEARNED:

Sketch what you saw:

RATE YOUR DAY:

TODAY'S FAVORITE MEMORY:

TODAY I AM GRATEFUL FOR:

Location:

DATE:

N
W · E
S

WEATHER:

TODAYS ACTIVITY:

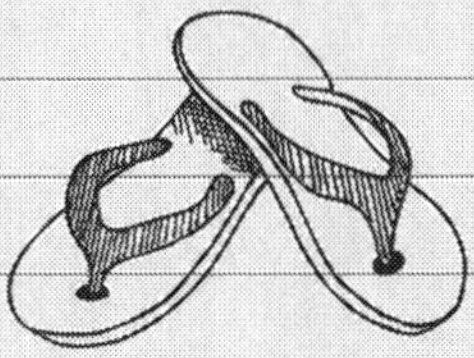

THE MOST INTERESTING I SAW:

TODAY I ATE:

TODAY I LEARNED:

Sketch what you saw:

RATE YOUR DAY:

TODAY'S FAVORITE MEMORY:

TODAY I AM GRATEFUL FOR:

Location: _____

DATE: _____

WEATHER:

N
W E
S

TODAYS ACTIVITY: _____
_____
_____
_____
_____
_____
_____

THE MOST INTERESTING I SAW: _____
_____
_____
_____

TODAY I ATE: _____
_____
_____
_____

TODAY I LEARNED: _____
_____
_____
_____
_____
_____
_____

Sketch what you saw:

RATE YOUR DAY:

TODAY'S FAVORITE MEMORY:

TODAY I AM GRATEFUL FOR:

Location: _____

DATE: _____

N
W E
S

WEATHER:

TODAYS ACTIVITY: _____

THE MOST INTERESTING I SAW: _____

TODAY I ATE: _____

TODAY I LEARNED: _____

Sketch what you saw:

RATE YOUR DAY:

TODAY'S FAVORITE MEMORY:

TODAY I AM GRATEFUL FOR:

Location:

DATE:

N
W E
S

WEATHER:

TODAYS ACTIVITY:

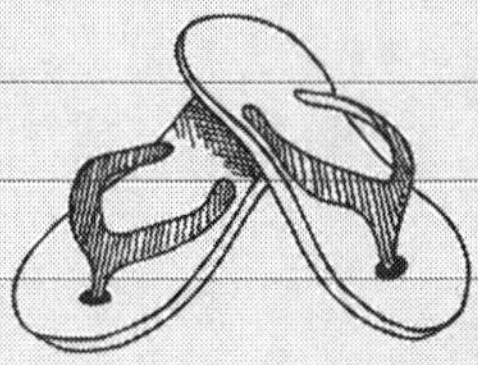

THE MOST INTERESTING I SAW:

TODAY I ATE:

TODAY I LEARNED:

Sketch what you saw:

RATE YOUR DAY:

TODAY'S FAVORITE MEMORY:

TODAY I AM GRATEFUL FOR:

Location: _____ DATE: _____

N
W E
S

WEATHER:

TODAYS ACTIVITY: _____

THE MOST INTERESTING I SAW: _____

TODAY I ATE: _____

TODAY I LEARNED: _____

Sketch what you saw:

RATE YOUR DAY:

TODAY'S FAVORITE MEMORY:

TODAY I AM GRATEFUL FOR:

Location: _____

DATE: _____

N
W · E
S

WEATHER:

TODAYS ACTIVITY: _____

THE MOST INTERESTING I SAW: _____

TODAY I ATE: _____

TODAY I LEARNED: _____

Sketch what you saw:

RATE YOUR DAY:

TODAY'S FAVORITE MEMORY:

TODAY I AM GRATEFUL FOR:

Location: _____

DATE: _____

_____

_____

WEATHER:

TODAYS ACTIVITY: _____

THE MOST INTERESTING I SAW: _____

TODAY I ATE: _____

TODAY I LEARNED: _____

Sketch what you saw:

RATE YOUR DAY:

TODAY'S FAVORITE MEMORY:

TODAY I AM GRATEFUL FOR:

Location: _____

DATE: _____

N
W E
S

WEATHER:

TODAYS ACTIVITY: _____

THE MOST INTERESTING I SAW: _____

TODAY I ATE: _____

TODAY I LEARNED: _____

Sketch what you saw:

RATE YOUR DAY:

TODAY'S FAVORITE MEMORY:

TODAY I AM GRATEFUL FOR:

Location:

DATE:

N
W E
S

WEATHER:

TODAYS ACTIVITY:

THE MOST INTERESTING I SAW:

TODAY I ATE:

TODAY I LEARNED:

Sketch what you saw:

RATE YOUR DAY:

TODAY'S FAVORITE MEMORY:

TODAY I AM GRATEFUL FOR:

Location:

DATE:

WEATHER:

N
W E
S

TODAYS ACTIVITY:

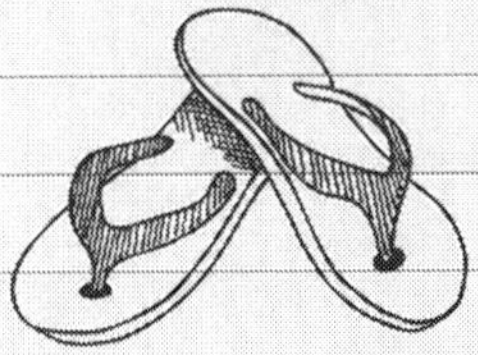

THE MOST INTERESTING I SAW:

TODAY I ATE:

TODAY I LEARNED:

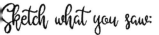

Sketch what you saw:

RATE YOUR DAY:

TODAY'S FAVORITE MEMORY:

TODAY I AM GRATEFUL FOR:

Location: ....

N
W   E
S

....
....
....

WEATHER:

TODAYS ACTIVITY: ....

THE MOST INTERESTING I SAW: ....

TODAY I ATE: ....

TODAY I LEARNED: ....

Sketch what you saw:

RATE YOUR DAY:

TODAY'S FAVORITE MEMORY:

TODAY I AM GRATEFUL FOR:

Location: _____

```
      N
  W ──┼── E
      S
```

WEATHER: ☀ ⛅ ☁ 🌧

TODAYS ACTIVITY: _____
_____
_____
_____
_____
_____

THE MOST INTERESTING I SAW: _____
_____
_____

TODAY I ATE: _____
_____
_____

TODAY I LEARNED: _____
_____
_____
_____
_____

Sketch what you saw:

RATE YOUR DAY:

TODAY'S FAVORITE MEMORY:

TODAY I AM GRATEFUL FOR:

Location: _____

DATE: _____

N
W E
S

WEATHER:

TODAYS ACTIVITY: _____

THE MOST INTERESTING I SAW: _____

TODAY I ATE: _____

TODAY I LEARNED: _____

Sketch what you saw:

RATE YOUR DAY:

TODAY'S FAVORITE MEMORY:

TODAY I AM GRATEFUL FOR:

Location: _____   DATE: _____

```
    N
 W ─╬─ E                                            WEATHER:
    S
```

_____

TODAYS ACTIVITY: _____

THE MOST INTERESTING I SAW: _____

TODAY I ATE: _____

TODAY I LEARNED: _____

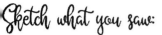
Sketch what you saw:

RATE YOUR DAY:

TODAY'S FAVORITE MEMORY:

TODAY I AM GRATEFUL FOR:

Location: _____

DATE: _____

N
W · E
S

WEATHER:

•••••••••••••••••••••••••••••••••••••••

TODAYS ACTIVITY: _____
_____
_____
_____
_____
_____

- - - - - - - - - - - - - - - - - - - -

THE MOST INTERESTING I SAW: _____
_____
_____
_____

- - - - - - - - - - - - - - - - - - - -

TODAY I ATE: _____
_____
_____
_____

- - - - - - - - - - - - - - - - - - - -

TODAY I LEARNED: _____
_____
_____
_____
_____

Sketch what you saw:

RATE YOUR DAY:

TODAY'S FAVORITE MEMORY:

TODAY I AM GRATEFUL FOR:

Location:

DATE:

N
W E
S

WEATHER:

TODAYS ACTIVITY:

THE MOST INTERESTING I SAW:

TODAY I ATE:

TODAY I LEARNED:

Sketch what you saw:

RATE YOUR DAY:

TODAY'S FAVORITE MEMORY:

TODAY I AM GRATEFUL FOR:

Location: _____

N
W   E
S

_____

_____

WEATHER:

TODAYS ACTIVITY: _____

THE MOST INTERESTING I SAW: _____

TODAY I ATE: _____

TODAY I LEARNED: _____

Sketch what you saw:

RATE YOUR DAY:

TODAY'S FAVORITE MEMORY:

TODAY I AM GRATEFUL FOR:

Location: _____

DATE: _____

N
W E
S

WEATHER:

TODAYS ACTIVITY: _____

THE MOST INTERESTING I SAW: _____

TODAY I ATE: _____

TODAY I LEARNED: _____

Sketch what you saw:

RATE YOUR DAY:

TODAY'S FAVORITE MEMORY:

TODAY I AM GRATEFUL FOR:

Location:

DATE:

N
W   E
S

WEATHER:

TODAYS ACTIVITY:

THE MOST INTERESTING I SAW:

TODAY I ATE:

TODAY I LEARNED:

Sketch what you saw:

RATE YOUR DAY:

TODAY'S FAVORITE MEMORY:

TODAY I AM GRATEFUL FOR:

Location:

N
W E
S

DATE:

WEATHER:

TODAYS ACTIVITY:

THE MOST INTERESTING I SAW:

TODAY I ATE:

TODAY I LEARNED:

Sketch what you saw:

RATE YOUR DAY:

TODAY'S FAVORITE MEMORY: _____

TODAY I AM GRATEFUL FOR: _____

Location:

DATE:

N
W E
S

WEATHER:

TODAYS ACTIVITY:

THE MOST INTERESTING I SAW:

TODAY I ATE:

TODAY I LEARNED:

Sketch what you saw:

RATE YOUR DAY:

TODAY'S FAVORITE MEMORY:

TODAY I AM GRATEFUL FOR:

Location: _____   DATE: _____

```
      N
W  ──┼──  E                                      WEATHER:
      S
```
_____

_____

TODAYS ACTIVITY: _____

_____

_____

_____

_____

THE MOST INTERESTING I SAW: _____

_____

_____

TODAY I ATE: _____

_____

_____

TODAY I LEARNED: _____

_____

_____

_____

_____

Sketch what you saw:

RATE YOUR DAY:

TODAY'S FAVORITE MEMORY:

TODAY I AM GRATEFUL FOR:

Location: _____ DATE: _____

N

W ⟡ E

S

WEATHER:

TODAYS ACTIVITY: _____

THE MOST INTERESTING I SAW: _____

TODAY I ATE: _____

TODAY I LEARNED: _____

Sketch what you saw:

RATE YOUR DAY:

TODAY'S FAVORITE MEMORY: _____

TODAY I AM GRATEFUL FOR: _____

Location:

DATE:

N
W E
S

WEATHER:

TODAYS ACTIVITY:

THE MOST INTERESTING I SAW:

TODAY I ATE:

TODAY I LEARNED:

Sketch what you saw:

RATE YOUR DAY:

TODAY'S FAVORITE MEMORY:

TODAY I AM GRATEFUL FOR:

Location:

DATE:

N
W E
S

WEATHER:

TODAYS ACTIVITY:

THE MOST INTERESTING I SAW:

TODAY I ATE:

TODAY I LEARNED:

Sketch what you saw:

RATE YOUR DAY:

TODAY'S FAVORITE MEMORY:

TODAY I AM GRATEFUL FOR:

Location:

DATE:

N
W E
S

WEATHER:

TODAYS ACTIVITY:

THE MOST INTERESTING I SAW:

TODAY I ATE:

TODAY I LEARNED:

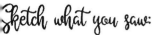

Sketch what you saw:

RATE YOUR DAY:

TODAY'S FAVORITE MEMORY:

TODAY I AM GRATEFUL FOR:

Location:

DATE:

WEATHER:

N
W E
S

TODAYS ACTIVITY:

THE MOST INTERESTING I SAW:

TODAY I ATE:

TODAY I LEARNED:

Sketch what you saw:

RATE YOUR DAY:

TODAY'S FAVORITE MEMORY:

TODAY I AM GRATEFUL FOR:

Location: _____

DATE: _____

N
W E
S

WEATHER:

TODAYS ACTIVITY: _____

THE MOST INTERESTING I SAW: _____

TODAY I ATE: _____

TODAY I LEARNED: _____

Sketch what you saw:

RATE YOUR DAY:

TODAY'S FAVORITE MEMORY:

TODAY I AM GRATEFUL FOR:

Location: _____

DATE: _____

N
W E
S

_____
_____

WEATHER:

☀ ⛅ ☁ 🌧

●●●●●●●●●●●●●●●●●●●●●●●●●●●●●●●●●●●●●●

TODAYS ACTIVITY: _____

THE MOST INTERESTING I SAW: _____

TODAY I ATE: _____

TODAY I LEARNED: _____

Sketch what you saw:

RATE YOUR DAY:

TODAY'S FAVORITE MEMORY:

TODAY I AM GRATEFUL FOR:

Location:

DATE: _____

WEATHER:

N
W E
S

TODAYS ACTIVITY:

THE MOST INTERESTING I SAW:

TODAY I ATE:

TODAY I LEARNED:

Sketch what you saw:

RATE YOUR DAY:

TODAY'S FAVORITE MEMORY:

TODAY I AM GRATEFUL FOR:

Location:

DATE:

WEATHER:

N
W E
S

TODAYS ACTIVITY:

THE MOST INTERESTING I SAW:

TODAY I ATE:

TODAY I LEARNED:

Sketch what you saw:

RATE YOUR DAY:

TODAY'S FAVORITE MEMORY:

TODAY I AM GRATEFUL FOR:

Location: _____

DATE: _____

N
W · E
S

WEATHER:

....

TODAYS ACTIVITY: _____

- - - - - - - - - - - - - - - - - - -

THE MOST INTERESTING I SAW: _____

- - - - - - - - - - - - - - - - - - -

TODAY I ATE: _____

- - - - - - - - - - - - - - - - - - -

TODAY I LEARNED: _____

Sketch what you saw:

RATE YOUR DAY:

TODAY'S FAVORITE MEMORY:

TODAY I AM GRATEFUL FOR:

Location:

DATE:

N
W · E
S

WEATHER:

TODAYS ACTIVITY:

THE MOST INTERESTING I SAW:

TODAY I ATE:

TODAY I LEARNED:

Sketch what you saw:

RATE YOUR DAY:

TODAY'S FAVORITE MEMORY:

TODAY I AM GRATEFUL FOR:

Location:

DATE:

WEATHER:

N
W E
S

TODAYS ACTIVITY:

THE MOST INTERESTING I SAW:

TODAY I ATE:

TODAY I LEARNED:

Sketch what you saw:

RATE YOUR DAY:

TODAY'S FAVORITE MEMORY:

TODAY I AM GRATEFUL FOR:

Made in United States
Orlando, FL
18 April 2022

16931081R00063